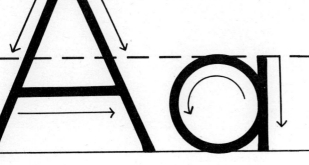

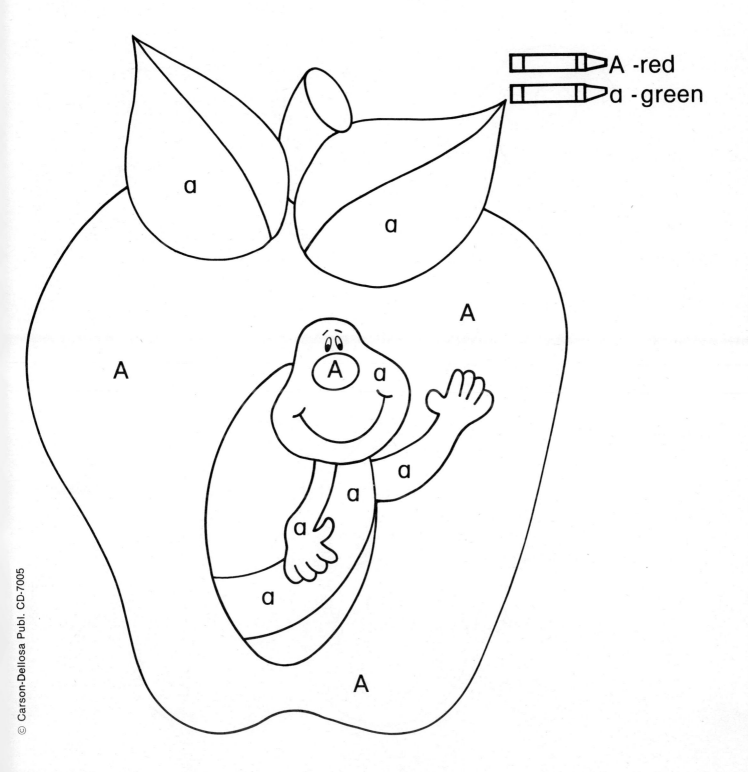

A -red
a -green

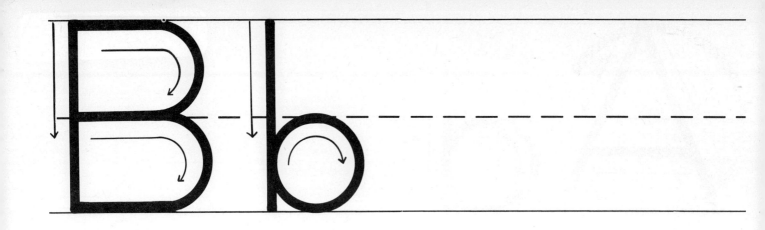

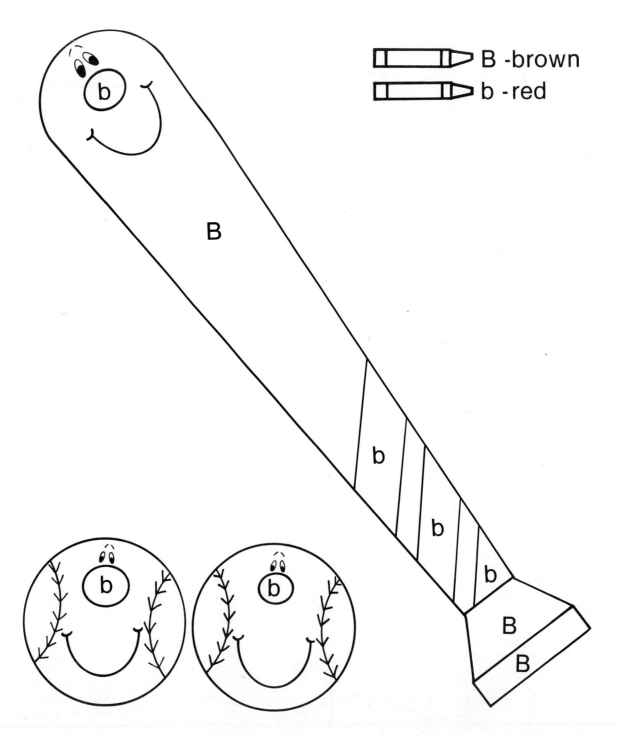

B -brown
b - red

C - brown
c - yellow

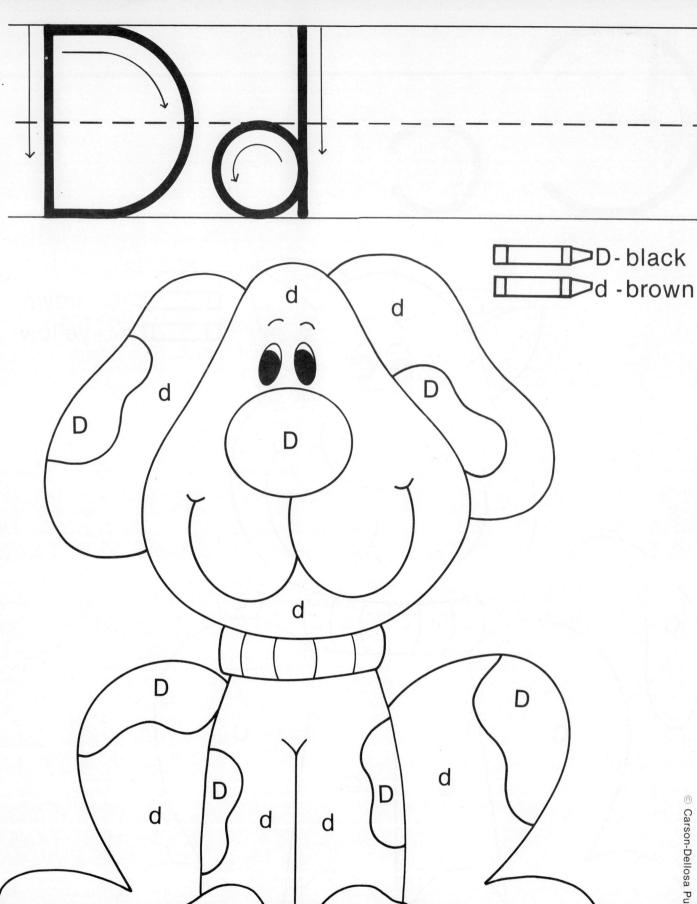

D - black
d - brown

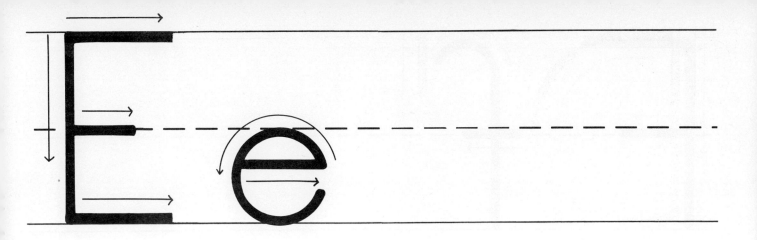

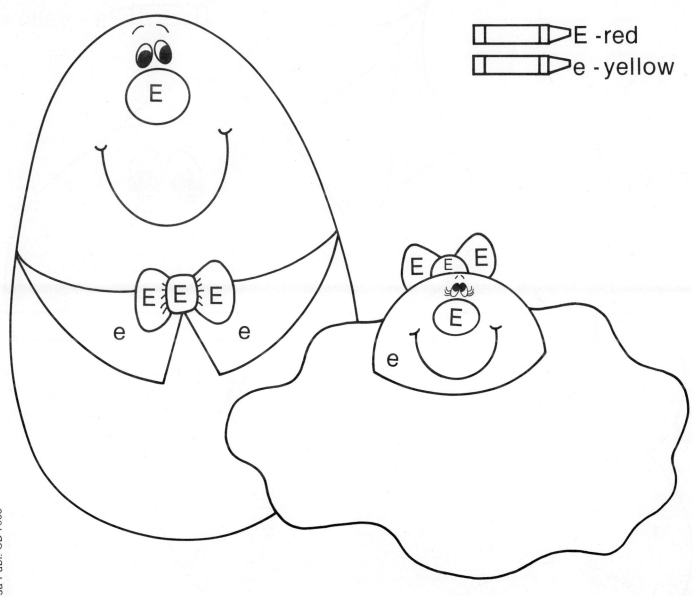

E - red
e - yellow

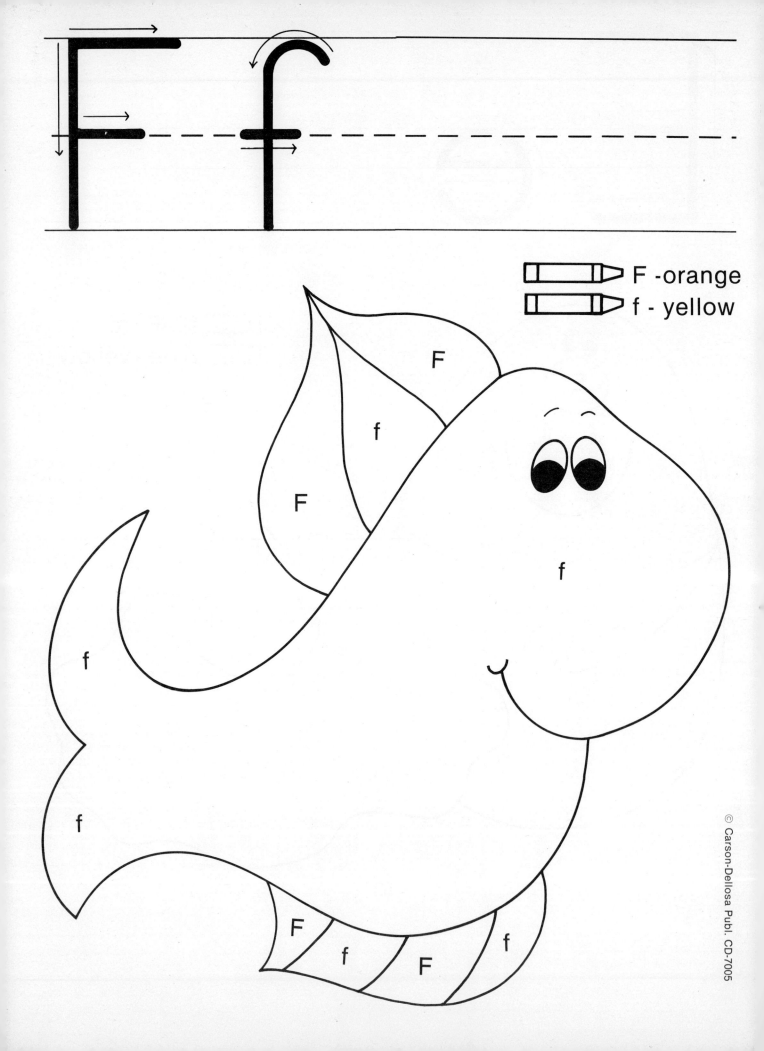

F -orange

f - yellow

G - orange
g - red

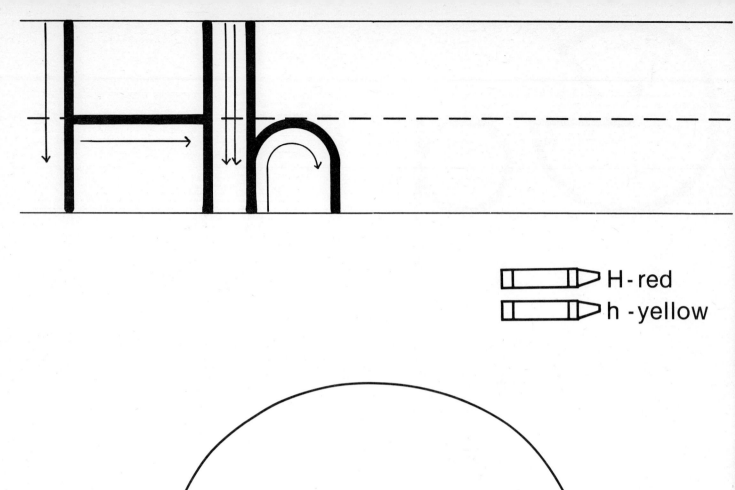

H-red
h-yellow

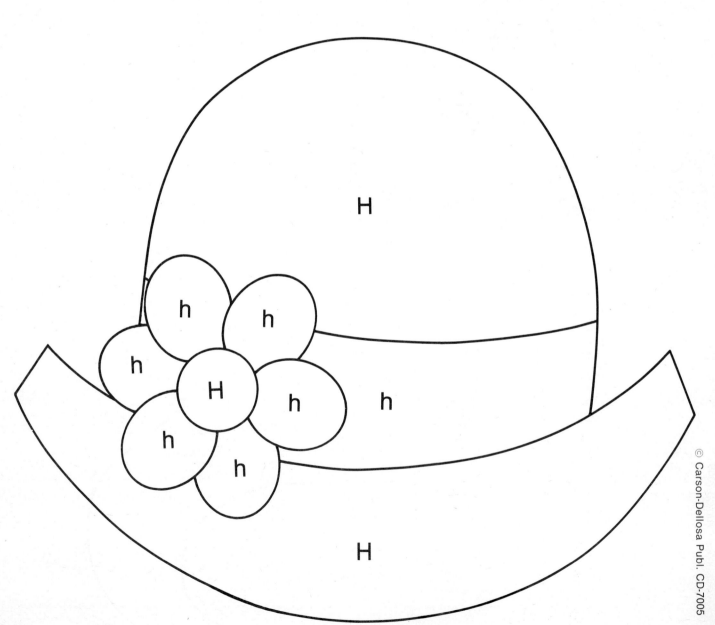

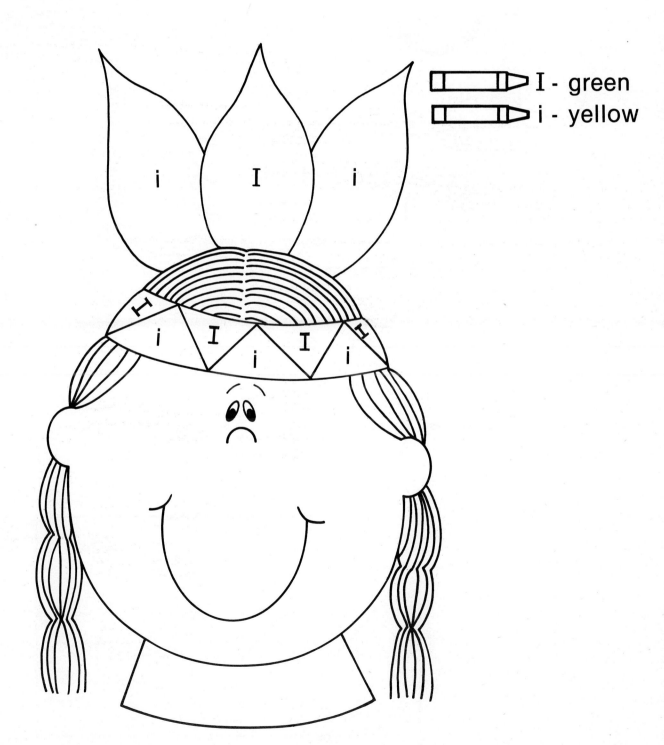

I - green
i - yellow

J - red
j - blue

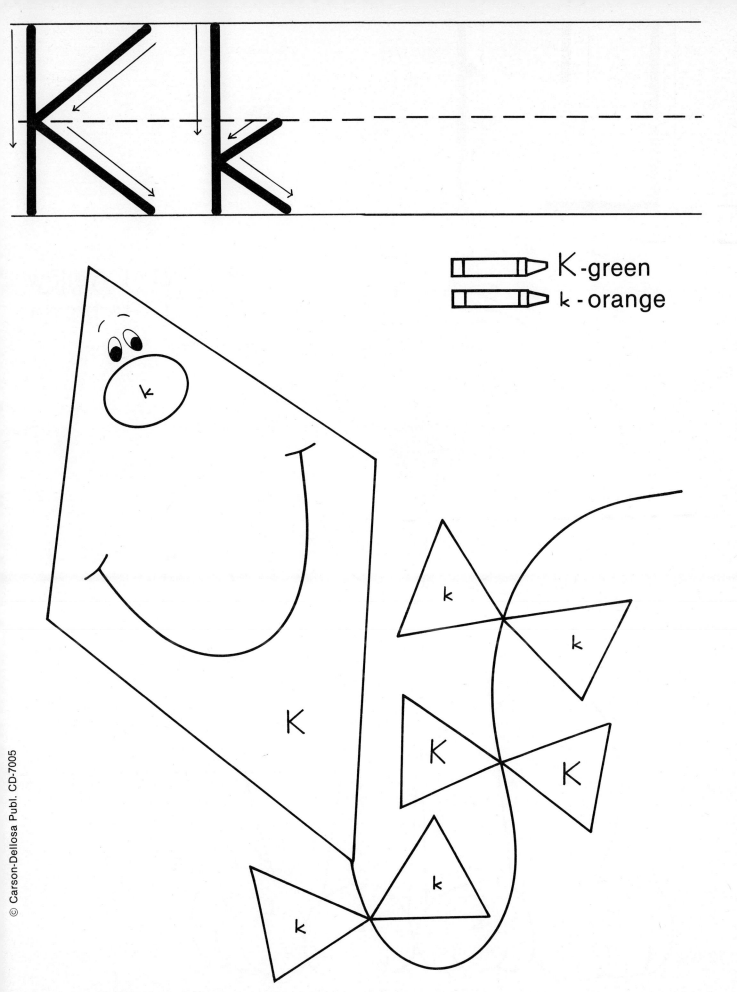

K -green

k - orange

L -yellow
l - brown

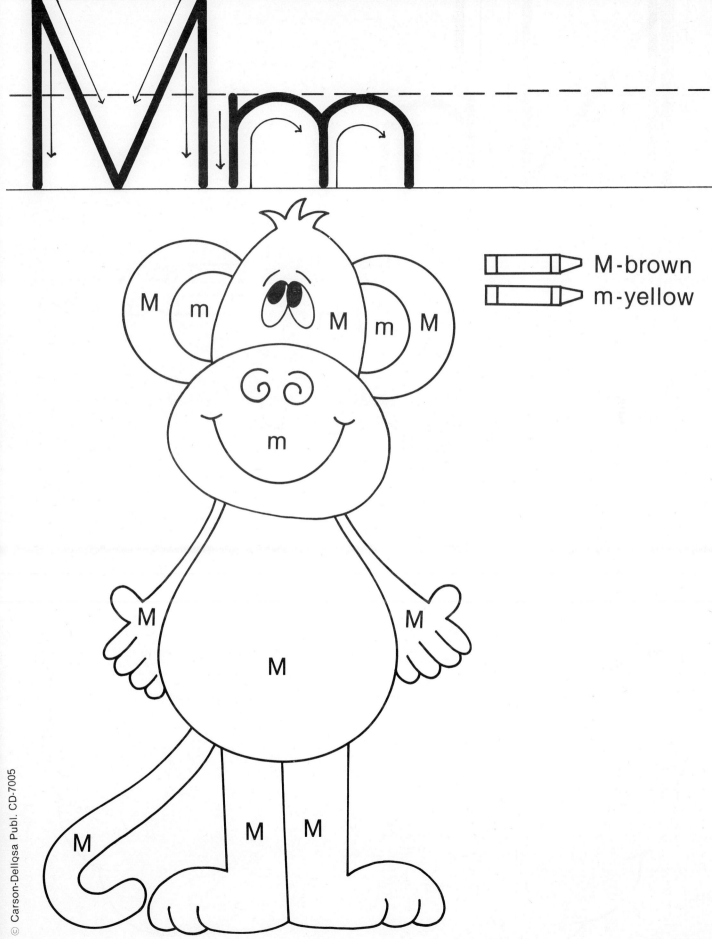

M-brown
m-yellow

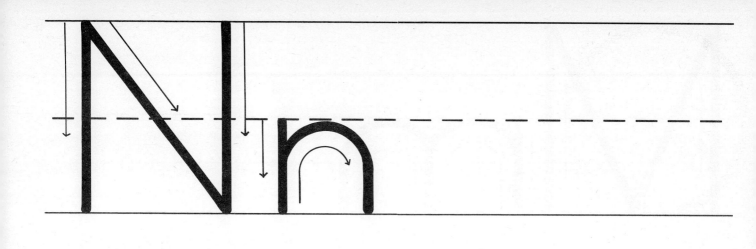

N-blue

n- yellow

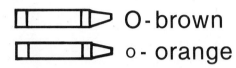

O- brown

o - orange

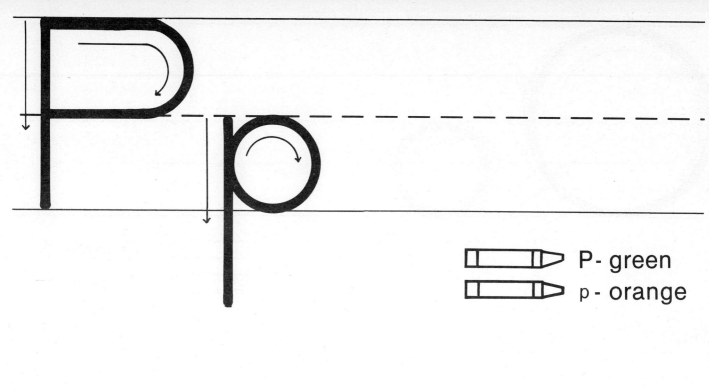

P- green
p - orange

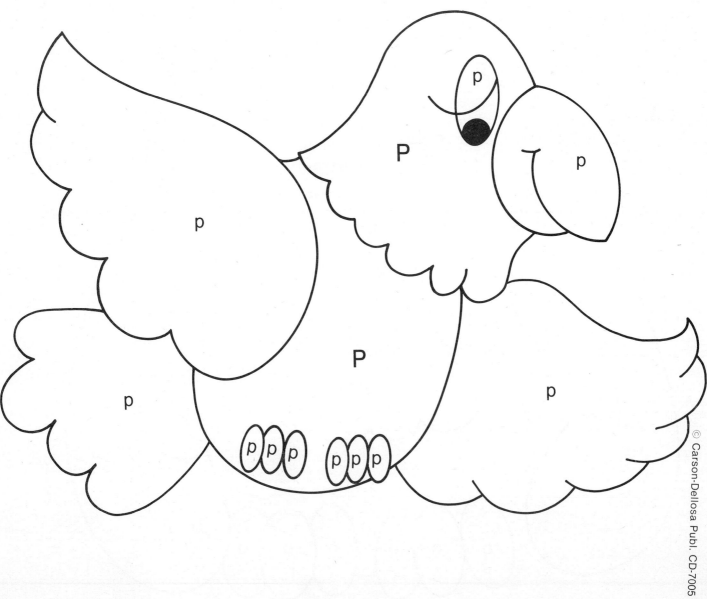

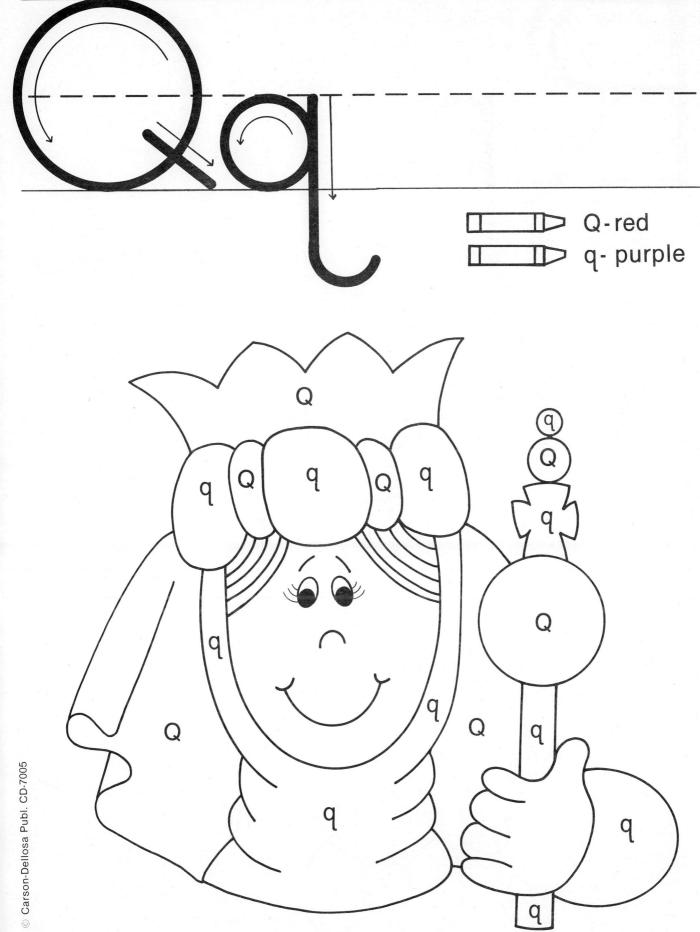

Q-red

q- purple

R r

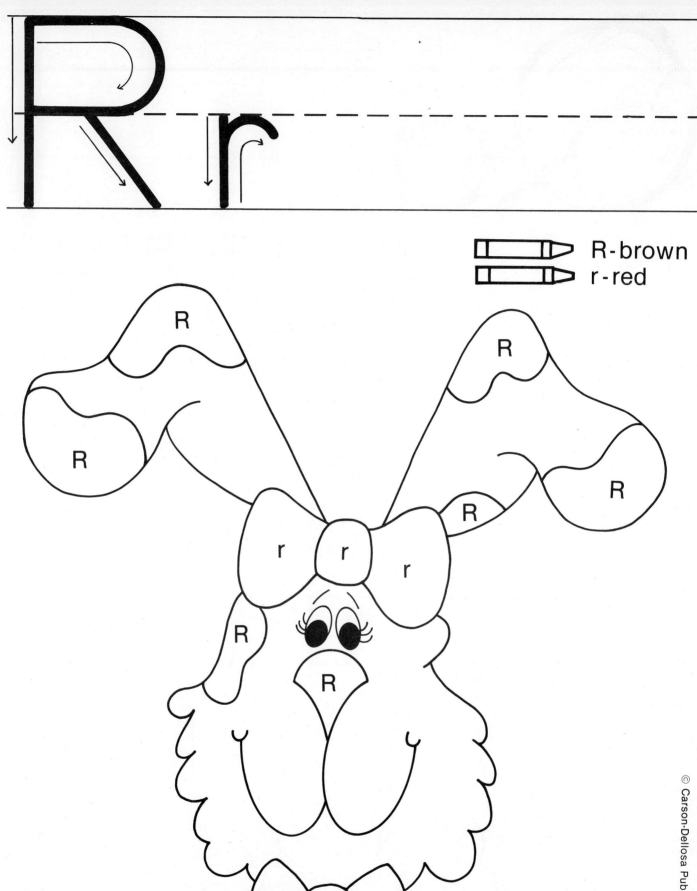

S s

S- orange
s - yellow

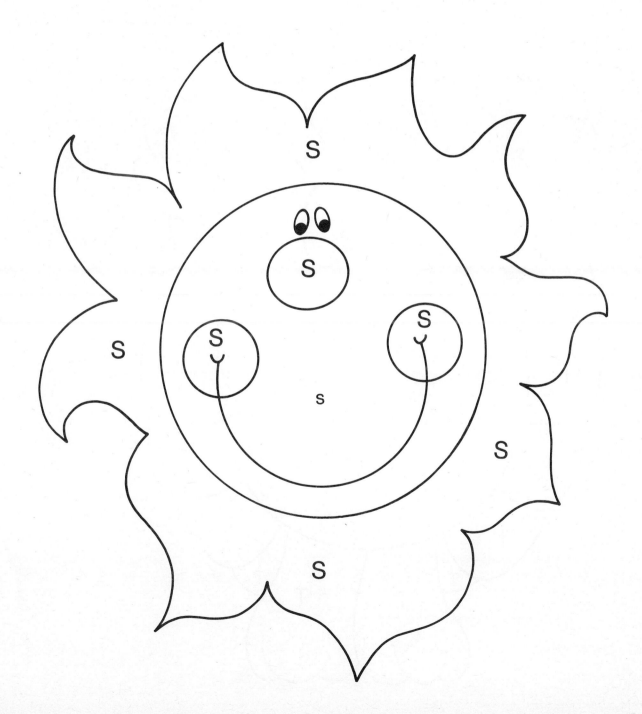

T- green
t- yellow

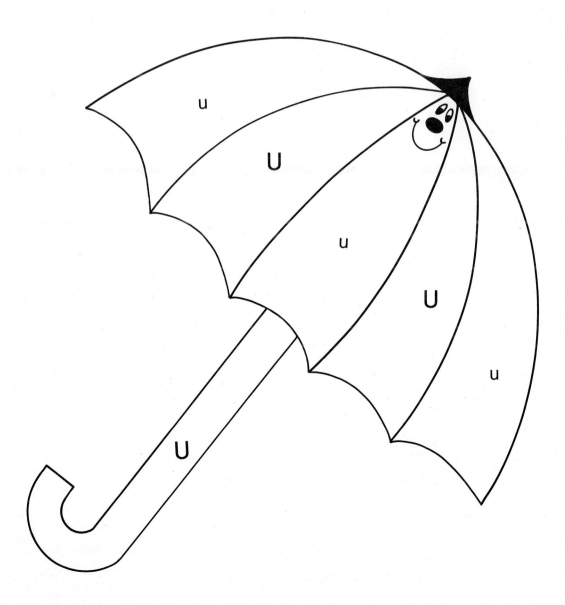

U - orange

u - green

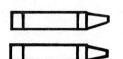

V - red
v - blue

W-green

w - yellow

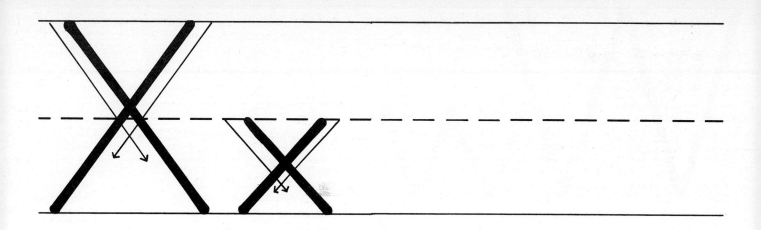

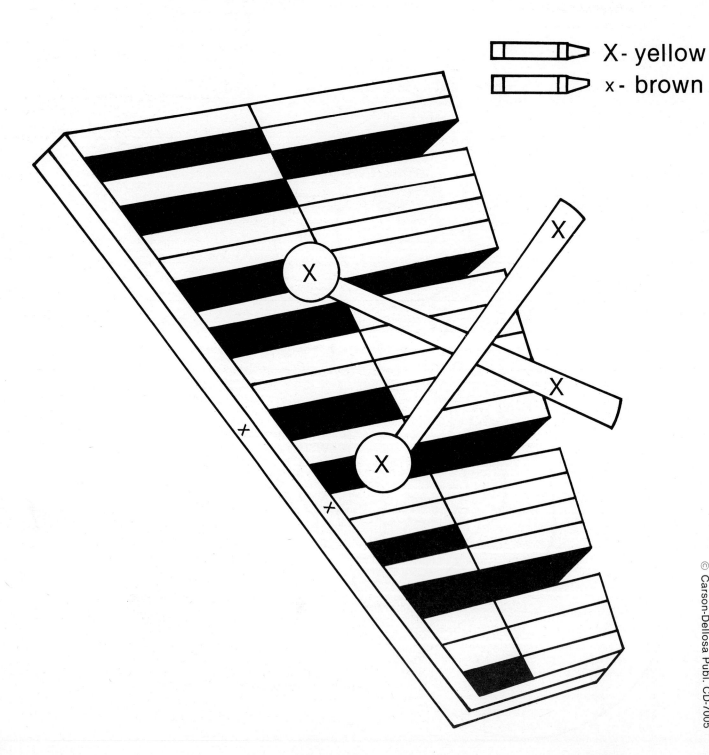

X- yellow

x- brown

Y- brown
y- yellow

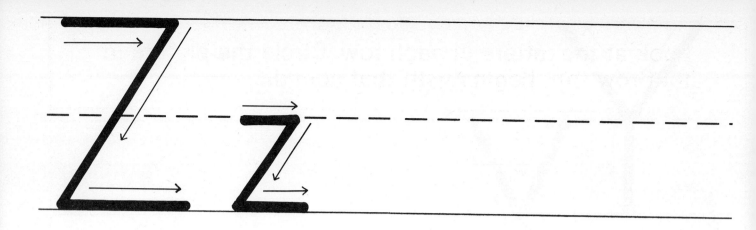

Z - red
z - black

Look at the letters in each row. Circle the picture in that row that begins with that sound.

Cc		
Gg		
Ee		
Kk	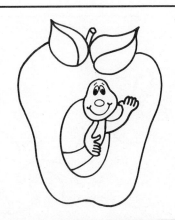	

Look at the letters in each row. Circle the picture in that row that begins with that sound.

Aa	 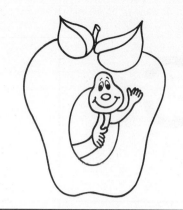
Ll	 
Ff	 
Bb	 

Look at the letters in each row. Circle the picture in that row that begins with that sound.

Pp	
Ss	
Ww	
Zz	

Draw a line to connect each picture to its beginning letter.

I i

R r

V v

B b

H h

T t

Draw a line to connect each picture to its beginning letter.

Qq

Ss

Uu

Pp

Yy

Nn

Draw a line to connect each picture to its beginning letter.

Oo

I i

Xx

Mm

Dd

Jj